MW01088774

Little
Hawaiian
Condiments
Cookbook

Cookbooks by Muriel Miura

Little
Hawaiian
Condiments
Cookbook

Recipes by Muriel Miura

Mutual Publishing

Photo Credits—
Photos by Kaz Tanabe: pg. 3, 7, 8, 10, 12, 14, 17, 18, 39, 44, 51, 55, 57, 60, 64, 66, 75
Photos from Dreamstime.com: pg. 5 © Krzysztof Slusarczyk; pg. 13 © Shariff Che' Lah;
pg. 15 © Maceofoto; pg. 16 © Andrzej Tokarski; pg. 19 © Mchudo; pg. 21, 32 © Jabiru; pg.
22 © Photoeuphoria; pg. 25 © Spaxia; pg 26 © Zkruger; pg. 27 © Vasiu; pg. 28 © Stuart
Monk; pg. 30 © Mchudo; pg. 31 © Paulwest5; pg. 34 © Svetlana Kolpakova; pg. 35 © Angelo
Gilardelli; pg. 36 © Design56; pg. 37, 40 © Vinicius Tupinamba; pg. 38 © Mblach; pg. 41 ©
Christian Draghici; pg. 43 © Johannes Gerhardus Swanepoel; pg. 46 © Valentyn75; pg. 48 ©
Jiri Hera; pg. 49 © Lukasz Olek ; pg. 52 © Le-thuy Do; pg. 53 © Christy Liem; pg. 54 © Luis
Louro; pg. 59 © Robyn Mackenzie; pg. 61 © Iwka; pg. 63 © Danny Smythe; pg. 67 © Viktorija
Kuprijanova; pg. 68 © Mchudo, © Vitaly Vasin; pg. 69 © Robstark; pg. 70 © Aleksandr
Ugorenkov; pg. 71 © Hmproudlove; pg. 72 © Dinoforlena; pg. 73 © Krzysztof Slusarczyk; pg.
76 © Motorolka; pg. 77 © Magdalena Bujak; pg. 78 © Oksix

ISBN-10: 1-56647-952-5
ISBN-13: 978-1-56647-952-3
Library of Congress Control Number: 2011932882

First Printing, September 2011

Mutual Publishing, LLC
1215 Center Street, Suite 210
Honolulu, Hawai'i 96816
Ph: 808-732-1709 / Fax: 808-734-4094
E-mail: info@mutualpublishing.com
www.mutualpublishing.com
Printed in Korea

Table of Contents

Dips

Dressings

Spreads

DIPS

California Dip

Makes about 2 cups

I've been told that all those great cocktail dips of today started with this recipe. It has been popular since about 1954.

1 envelope (1-3/4 oz.) onion soup mix
2 cups (16 oz.) sour cream

In a small bowl blend onion soup mix with sour cream; chill. Serve with crackers or crudités.

Variations:
- **California Vegetable Dip:** Add 1 green pepper, chopped; 1 tomato, chopped; and 2 teaspoons chili powder.
- **Bleu Cheese Dip:** Add 1/4 pound bleu cheese, crumbled, and 1/4 cup finely chopped macadamia nuts or walnuts.
- **Shrimp Dip:** Add 1 cup finely chopped cooked shrimp and 1/4 cup ketchup.
- **Clam Dip:** Add 1 can (7-1/2 oz.) minced clams, drained, and 2 tablespoons chili sauce.

—*Originally appeared in* Hawai'i Cooks & Saves

Clam Dip

Makes about 2 cups

1 package (8 oz.) cream cheese, softened
2 tablespoons mayonnaise
6 tablespoons clam liquid
3/4 teaspoon
Worcestershire sauce
1/2 teaspoon salt
2 tablespoons minced onion
1 can (7 oz.) minced clams, drained

Cream together cream cheese, mayonnaise, and clam liquid.
Stir in remaining ingredients. Chill.

—*Originally appeared in* Hawai'i's Party Food

All-Purpose Dip

Makes about 1-1/4 cups

1/4 cup dairy sour cream
1/4 cup canola oil
1/2 cup grated cheddar cheese
2 tablespoons minced onion

Combine ingredients and mix. Serve as a dip with raw vegetables, a spread on assorted crackers, or as a salad dressing.

—*Originally appeared in* Hawai'i's Party Food

Curry Dip

Makes about 1 cup

1 cup dairy sour cream
2 tablespoons mayonnaise
1/4 teaspoon garlic salt
1-1/4 teaspoons curry powder

Blend all ingredients together thoroughly. Chill and serve with vegetables or chips.

—*Originally appeared in* Hawai'i's Party Food

Spicy Polynesian Avocado Dip

Makes abut 2 cups

1 medium avocado
1 teaspoon lemon juice
1/4 teaspoon Worcestershire sauce
2 tablespoons curry powder
1/4 teaspoon garlic salt
Dash cayenne pepper
1 tablespoon sugar
2 tablespoons macadamia nuts, chopped
2 tablespoons crumbled crisp bacon

Cut avocado in half; remove seed and skin. Mash avocado with a fork, not too smooth. Combine with all remaining ingredients and mix well.

Note: If dip is not to be used immediately, cover with foil to prevent darkening of the avocado.

—*Originally appeared in* Hawai'i's Party Food

'Ahi Poke Dip

Makes about 3-1/2 cups

1-3/4 cups mayonnaise
1/4 cup minced pickled ginger (gari shoga)
1/2 cup minced green onion
1/2 cup cilantro
3 tablespoons toasted sesame seeds
1/4 cup fresh lemon juice
1/3 cup soy sauce
1/3 cup finely minced fresh 'ahi
Shichimi togarashi (chili pepper) or red pepper flakes to taste

---

Combine all ingredients except 'ahi and pepper in blender jar or food processor and mix until smooth. Refrigerate until ready to use. Add 'ahi and pepper just before serving; mix well. Delicious on toasted bread rounds or crackers.

—*Originally appeared in* Hawai'i's Party Food

Oriental Ginger Dip

Makes about 2 cups

1 cup mayonnaise, chilled
1 cup dairy sour cream
1/4 cup finely chopped onion
2 tablespoons minced parsley
1/4 cup minced water chestnuts
1 tablespoon minced candied ginger
1 clove garlic, minced
1 tablespoon soy sauce

Combine mayonnaise and sour cream. Stir in remaining ingredients. Serve with sesame seed crackers or potato chips.

—*Originally appeared in* Hawai'i's Party Food

Hawaiian
Bleu Cheese Dip

Makes about 2 cups

1 package (8 oz.) cream cheese, softened
1 package (4 oz.) bleu cheese, softened
2 tablespoons chopped chives
1 teaspoon dill weed
1 teaspoon seasoned salt
1/4 teaspoon garlic powder
1 can (8-1/4 oz.) crushed pineapple

Fresh raw vegetables or apple wedges

Beat together cream and bleu cheese until light and fluffy. Beat in chives, dill weed, seasoned salt, and garlic powder until well blended. Fold in pineapple and syrup; mix well. Chill 1 to 2 hours before serving. Serve with raw vegetables or apple wedges.

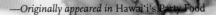

—*Originally appeared in* Hawai'i's Party Food

Hot Crab Dip

Makes about 2 cups

1 package (8 oz.) cream cheese, softened
1 can (7-1/2 oz.) crabmeat, drained
1 tablespoon milk
1/2 teaspoon Worcestershire sauce
1/2 cup minced green onion or chives
1 tablespoon chopped macadamia nuts

Combine all ingredients and beat until light and fluffy. Bake.
Temperature: 350°F. Time: 10 minutes.

—*Originally appeared in* Hawai'i's Party Food

Green Goddess Dip

Makes about 2-1/2 cups

1 clove garlic, grated
2 tablespoons anchovy paste
3 tablespoons finely chopped chives
1 tablespoon lemon juice
1 tablespoon tarragon wine vinegar
1/2 cup heavy sour cream
1 cup mayonnaise
1/3 cup finely chopped parsley
Hawaiian rock salt to taste
Dash fresh ground black pepper to taste

Combine ingredients in order given. Pour into serving bowl and chill. Mix well just before serving.

—*Originally appeared in* Hawai'i's Party Food

DRESSINGS

Basic French Dressing

Makes 2 cups

2 teaspoons salt
1 teaspoon sugar
1/2 teaspoon white pepper
1 teaspoon paprika
1/2 cup vinegar or lemon juice
1-1/2 cups canola oil

Combine all ingredients in a jar. Cover and shake well. Refrigerate before using.

Variations:
- **Bleu Cheese:** Add 1/2 cup crumbled bleu cheese.
- **Celery Seed:** Add 1/4 cup ketchup, 3 tablespoons sugar, 1 teaspoon celery seed, 1 clove crushed garlic.
- **Curry:** Add 1/2 teaspoon curry powder.
- **Herb:** 2-1/2 tablespoons chopped parsley, 1/2 tablespoon powdered thyme, 2 teaspoons oregano.
- **Honey:** Add 3 tablespoons lemon juice, 3 tablespoons honey, 3 tablespoons sugar, 1 teaspoon grated lemon rind.

—Originally appeared in Homemade Gifts of Sweets & Treats

Honey Mustard Dressing

Makes about 1-1/2 cups

3 egg yolks
1/3 cup fresh ginger, chopped
2 tablespoons soy sauce
2 tablespoons rice wine vinegar
1 teaspoon sesame oil
3/4 cup honey
1 teaspoon salt
2 Hawaiian chili peppers, seeded
1 tablespoon Dijon mustard
1-1/2 cups vegetable or olive oil
2 tablespoons water
Juice of 1 lemon

In an electric blender, blend egg yolks, ginger, and soy sauce together for 10 seconds. Add next six ingredients; blend at low speed and slowly add the oil. As the mixture thickens, add the water, then lemon juice. May be refrigerated in covered jar for up to 2 weeks.

—*Originally appeared in* Homemade Gifts of Sweets & Treats

Miso Dressing

Makes 2-1/2 cups

1 cup canola oil
1/4 cup sesame oil
1 clove garlic
1 tablespoon chopped round onion
1/4 cup toasted sesame seeds
3/4 cup sugar
3 tablespoons miso
1 tablespoon lime juice
1 teaspoon dry mustard
1/2 cup mayonnaise

Blend all ingredients in blender or food processor. Store in covered jar in refrigerator.

—Originally appeared in Homemade Gifts of Sweets & Treats

Chili Sauce Dressing

Makes about 2-1/2 cups

1 cup chili sauce
1/2 cup olive oil
1/2 cup red vinegar
1/4 cup celery, minced
2 cloves garlic, minced
2 teaspoons oregano
1-1/2 teaspoons black pepper, freshly ground
1-1/2 teaspoons salt
3 tablespoons sugar

Combine all ingredients in a blender; mix on high speed
until well blended. Store in tightly covered jars in refrigerator.

Originally appeared in Homemade Gifts of Sweets & Treats

Citrus Vinaigrette
Makes 2 cups

1/2 cup fresh orange juice
1/4 cup rice vinegar
1-1/2 tablespoons fresh lime juice
1-1/2 tablespoons fresh lemon juice
1 shallot, peeled and chopped
1/2 teaspoon black pepper, freshly ground
1/4 teaspoon salt
1 cup olive oil

Combine the orange juice, rice vinegar, lime and lemon juices, shallot, pepper, and salt in a food processor. Blend well. Add the oil slowly, processing until emulsion is formed. Serve over greens and fruit of your choice.

—*Originally appeared in* Homemade Gifts of Sweets & Treats

Mixed Herb Vinegar

Makes 2 cups

1 cup chopped mixed fresh herbs (rosemary, oregano, fennel, and basil)
2 cups white wine or cider vinegar

Place herbs and vinegar in wide-necked jar. Cover with vinegar-proof lid and leave in warm place for 2 weeks; shake jar daily. Strain vinegar through cheesecloth. Place a sprig of herbs in clean 1-pint bottle; pour in vinegar and seal with vinegar-proof lid.

Variations:
- **English Herb Vinegar:** Use 1/4 cup chopped fresh sage and 1/3 cup chopped fresh thyme in place of mixed herbs. Place a sprig of sage and thyme in 1-pint bottle with strained vinegar. Seal with vinegar-proof lid.
- **Tarragon Vinegar:** Use 2/3 cup chopped tarragon in place of mixed herbs. Place sprig of tarragon in the 1-pint bottle with strained vinegar. Seal with vinegar-proof lid.
- **Other Herb Vinegar:** Red or green basil, oregano, wild thyme, peppercorns, mint, rosemary, dill, chervil, chive blossoms, or combinations of these and others.

—Originally appeared in Homemade Gifts of Sweets & Treats

Russian Dressing

Makes 2 cups

3 cloves garlic
1 cup vegetable oil
1/2 cup ketchup
1/2 cup sugar
1/2 cup vinegar
1-inch slice of onion
3 teaspoons fresh parsley
1 teaspoon fresh oregano
1 teaspoon fresh basil
1/2 teaspoon dry mustard
1/4 teaspoon celery seed
Salt and freshly ground pepper to taste

Mince garlic in a food processor; add remaining ingredients
and blend until smooth. Pour into jars; cover and refrigerate.
Serve over a salad of greens.

—*Originally appeared in* Homemade Gifts of Sweets & Treats

Roquefort or Bleu Cheese Dressing

Makes about 1-1/2 cups

1-1/4 ounce Roquefort or bleu cheese
1/2 cup mayonnaise
1 cup sour cream
2 tablespoons canola oil
1 teaspoon garlic salt
1/4 teaspoon freshly ground pepper

Combine all ingredients in a jar; cover
tightly and shake vigorously. Chill until
ready to use.

—*Originally appeared in* Hawai'i's Party Food

Thousand Island

Makes about 1-1/4 cups

1 cup mayonnaise
2 tablespoons chili sauce
1 tablespoon sweet pickle relish
1 tablespoon chopped onion
1 tablespoon chopped green onions
1 hard-cooked egg, chopped

Combine all ingredients in a bowl and mix until well blended. Chill before serving with salad greens.

Variations:
- **Louis Dressing:** Decrease mayonnaise to 1/2 cup and increase chili sauce to 3/4 cup and add 1/4 teaspoon Worcestershire sauce and salt to taste. Omit relish, onion, pepper, and egg. Great with seafood.
- **Russian Dressing:** Increase chili sauce to 1/4 cup and add 1 teaspoon prepared horseradish. Omit egg.

—*Originally appeared in* Homemade Gifts of Sweets & Treats

Sesame Dressing

Makes 2 cups

2 tablespoons sesame oil
3/4 cup canola oil
1 teaspoon salt
1 clove garlic, pressed
1/4 cup onions, finely chopped
1/2 cup lemon juice
1/4 cup honey
2 tablespoons toasted sesame seeds

Blend all ingredients except for 1 tablespoon sesame seeds in a food processor or blender. Stir in remaining sesame seeds. Pour into jars; cover and refrigerate.

—*Originally appeared in* Homemade Gifts of Sweets & Treats

Papaya Seed Dressing

Makes about 1-1/2 cups

1 cup canola oil
1/4 cup tarragon vinegar
1 tablespoon lemon juice
1/4 cup sugar
1/2 teaspoon salt
1/2 teaspoon dry mustard
1 tablespoon minced onion
1-1/2 tablespoons fresh papaya seeds

Put oil, vinegar, lemon juice, sugar, salt, mustard, and onion in blender jar; cover and blend on high for 2 minutes. Add papaya seeds and blend until seeds are the size of coarsely ground pepper. Serve over crisp greens.

—*Originally appeared in* Hawai'i's Party Food

SPREADS

Jams, Jellies, Marmalades, Butters, & Chutneys

Mango Jam

Makes 1 pint

8 cups ripe mango slices
2 cups water
2 cups sugar
2 tablespoons lemon juice

Cook mango slices in water over low heat until tender. Press through strainer. Add sugar and lemon juice; cook slowly over low heat until of desired consistency for jam. Pack in hot sterilized jars and seal with paraffin, or place in refrigerator for immediate use.

—*Originally appeared in* Homemade Gifts of Sweets & Treats

Papaya Pineapple Jam

Makes about 6 to 7 quarts

2 cups pineapple, crushed or chopped
2 cups papaya, chopped
4 cups sugar
1/4 cup lemon juice

Combine all ingredients in large saucepan; stir to blend well. Bring to a boil then lower heat and cook slowly, stirring constantly to prevent burning for about 1-1/2 to 2 hours. Pour into hot sterilized jars and seal with paraffin.

Note: Firm-ripe or under-ripe fruit should be used for jelly. Pectin and acid content decrease as the fruit ripens. Use overripe fruits for butter, jam, or marmalade.

—*Originally appeared in* Homemade Gifts of Sweets & Treats

Guava Jam

Makes 8 (8-ounce) jars

8 large firm-ripe guavas
1 cup water
Sugar

Wash guavas; trim off blossom ends. Cut guavas into large cubes. Put 1/3 of the guava cubes and 1/3 cup water into a blender. Cover and blend at high speed until smooth, turning blender on and off when necessary to draw food down into the blades. Repeat until all of the guavas and water are blended; strain to remove seeds. Measure pulp into a large saucepan; add an equal amount of sugar. Cook over medium heat until mixture reaches jam consistency, about 30 minutes.

Sterilize jars. Remove jam from heat. Pour into hot jars. Seal with 1/4-inch layer melted paraffin while jam is hot. Cool 5 to 10 minutes, pour spoonful of melted paraffin on top and tilt jars so paraffin runs 1/4-inch up sides of jars. Cool completely. Cover with lid.

—*Originally appeared in* Holiday Gift-Giving Recipes

Pineapple Jelly

Makes about 8 (8-ounce) jars

This easy-to-make jelly reminds me of fine marmalade.

1 lime
1 can (6 oz.) frozen concentrated pineapple juice
1 can frozen concentrated pineapple-grapefruit* juice
1 package (1-3/4 oz.) dry pectin
2-1/2 cups water
5-1/2 cups sugar
1/4 teaspoon ground ginger
Hot paraffin wax for sealing

Pare peel of lime very thinly, being careful not to get any white layer of rind; cut into very thin 1-inch slivers; set aside. Squeeze juice and reserve. Combine frozen juices with pectin and water in large saucepan; cook over medium-high heat, stirring constantly, until bubbles form around the edge. Add sugar, ginger, lime peel, and lime juice all at once; bring to a full rolling boil. Boil 1 minute, stirring constantly. Remove from heat; skim. Pour into sterilized 8-ounce jelly jars. Seal with hot paraffin. Allow paraffin to cool before covering with lid.

*May use frozen concentrated pineapple-orange juice instead.

—*Originally appeared in* Homemade Gifts of Sweets & Treats

Coffee Jelly

Serves 4

This is an old-fashioned dessert that has recently sprung up again on the menus of some of O'ahu's eateries.

1 package unflavored gelatin
1/4 cup water
1-1/2 cups strong freshly brewed coffee
1 tablespoon Kahlua, optional
1 cup heavy cream or sweetened
   whipped cream
1 tablespoon Hawaiian raw sugar

Sprinkle gelatin over water; let stand 2 to 3 minutes. Pour hot coffee over softened gelatin and stir until gelatin dissolves completely. Add Kahlua, if desired. Pour into individual cups and refrigerate until firm, about 2 hours. Pour cold heavy cream over congealed gelatin to cover and top with sprinkle of 1 teaspoon sugar or top gelatin with dollop of sweetened whipped cream. Serve immediately.

—Originally appeared in Homemade Gifts of Sweets & Treats

Passion Fruit Jelly

Makes 4 (6-ounce) jars

1 cup water
3-1/4 cups sugar
1 (3 oz.) pouch liquid pectin
3 tablespoons lemon juice
1 (6 oz.) can frozen passion fruit juice, thawed

Sterilize jars. In a saucepan, combine water and sugar. Bring
to a boil and boil for 1 minute, stirring constantly. Remove
from heat and immediately stir in pectin. Stir in juices. Skim
foam and pour into hot jars. Seal with melted paraffin while
jelly is hot.

—Originally appeared in
Homemade Gifts of Sweets & Treats

Pineapple Orange Marmalade

Makes about 3-1/4 quarts

3 oranges, seeded and thinly sliced crosswise
1 lemon, seeded and thinly sliced crosswise
2 (16-ounce) cans crushed pineapple in syrup
8 cups sugar

Quarter each citrus fruit slice. Place fruits in large saucepan; add water to cover. Simmer 45 minutes or until peel is soft. Add pineapple and syrup; simmer 15 minutes. Add sugar; stir until sugar dissolves. Bring to a boil and cook rapidly for 20 to 25 minutes, or until marmalade reaches 221°F. Remove from heat; let stand 10 minutes. Stir well; ladle hot marmalade into hot sterilized jars. Wipe rim of jar with a clean damp cloth; seal and cover. Store in cool place.

Sealing jars: Wash and dry jars, lids, and bands. Place jars on rack in large pot. Place lids in saucepan; cover jars and lids with water. Bring both pans to a boil; boil 10 minutes. Drain jars; fill to within 1/4 inch of tops. Wipe jar rims and threads. Quickly cover with lids and screw bands on tightly. Invert jars 5 minutes; turn upright. Sealed jars should be refrigerated unless sealed with melted paraffin.

—Originally appeared in Homemade Gifts of Sweets & Treats

Kumquat Marmalade

Makes 8 pints

3 quarts water
2 cups (about 24) kumquats, seeded and thinly sliced
1-1/4 cups orange pulp, chopped
1-1/4 cups orange peel, sliced
1/2 cup lemon juice
9 cups sugar

Combine water and fruit in saucepan. Cover and let stand in a cool place overnight, then bring to a boil and cook until peel is tender. To each cup of fruit mixture add 1 cup sugar. Stir until sugar is dissolved. Cook rapidly and keep testing for jelly, about 45 minutes, stirring occasionally to prevent sticking. Pour immediately into hot jars, seal with paraffin.

Syrupy jelly may be caused by too much sugar; undercooking; or cooking very acetic juice and sugar for too long.

—Originally appeared in Homemade Gifts of Sweets & Treats

Basil Butter
Makes 1/2 cup

1/2 cup butter, softened
8 fresh basil leaves, minced

Beat butter and basil together until creamy. Press into butter mold or roll into cylinder; cover with plastic wrap and chill until firm.

—Originally appeared in Homemade Gifts of Sweets & Treats

Garlic Butter
Makes 1/2 cup

1/2 cup butter, softened
4 cloves garlic, pressed
1/4 teaspoon white pepper
1 tablespoon fresh parsley, minced

Combine all ingredients; beat until butter is creamy. Press into butter mold; chill until firm.

—Originally appeared in Homemade Gifts of Sweets & Treats

Wasabi Butter

Makes 1/2 cup

1/2 cup butter, softened
1/2 teaspoon wasabi powder
1/4 teaspoon water

Combine wasabi powder and water; mix until smooth adding more water if necessary to form paste consistency. Add wasabi paste to butter and beat until creamy. Press into butter mold; chill until firm.

—Originally appeared in
Homemade Gifts of Sweets & Treats

Banana Chutney

Makes about 1 pint

8 large ripe bananas, peeled and thinly sliced
1 pound onions, finely chopped
1-1/4 cups dates, pitted and chopped
1/2 cup crystallized ginger, chopped
2-1/2 cups cider vinegar
1-1/2 cups light brown sugar, packed
1 tablespoon salt
1 tablespoon mixed pickling spice

Mix bananas, onions, dates, ginger, vinegar, sugar, and salt in a large saucepan. Tie pickling spice in a 6-inch square of cheesecloth. Suspend in pan so spices are immersed in liquid; bring to a boil. Reduce heat to low; simmer 1 hour or until thick and golden brown, stirring frequently. Remove pickling spice. Ladle hot chutney into hot sterilized jars and seal with paraffin. Wipe rim of jar with clean damp cloth; cover and store in cool place. Let mature 1 month before using.

—*Originally appeared in* Homemade Gifts of Sweets & Treats

Mango Chutney

Makes 6 to 8 cups

12 cups green mango slices
2 tablespoons Hawaiian rock salt
2 cups vinegar
1/2 cup water
4 cups granulated sugar
2 cups brown sugar, packed
1 cup raisins, optional
1/4 cup ginger root, chopped
1 small onion, chopped
3 cloves garlic, minced or crushed
2-1/2 tablespoons (7–8) hot chili peppers, minced
1/2 teaspoon ground cinnamon
1/4 teaspoon ground cloves
1/4 teaspoon nutmeg, optional
1/4 teaspoon allspice, optional

Sprinkle salt over mango slices and let stand overnight. Rinse and drain.

Combine sugars with vinegar and water; bring to a boil. Add remaining ingredients, except mangoes, and cook 15 minutes. Add mangoes; simmer over low heat 30 to 45 minutes or until of desired consistency, stirring frequently to prevent sticking. Pour into hot sterilized jars and seal with paraffin.

—*Originally appeared in* Homemade Gifts of Sweets & Treats

SALSAS

Fresh Tomato Salsa

Makes about 3-1/2 cups

This fresh tomato-based salsa adds excitement to everything it touches—taco chips, fish, eggs and meat. It is a staple of southwestern cooking plus you have a delicious dip that's low in calories.

3 medium tomatoes, seeded and chopped
1/2 cup minced green onion
1/4 cup chopped green bell pepper
3 tablespoons lime juice
2-1/2 tablespoons chopped fresh cilantro
1 tablespoon finely chopped jalapeño chilies
1/2 teaspoon salt
2 cloves garlic, minced

Mix all ingredients and serve with tortilla chips, crackers or vegetables.

—*Originally appeared in*
Hawai'i Cooks & Saves

Lychee Salsa

Makes 6 to 8 servings

1 cup lychee fruit, fresh or canned
1/2 cup fresh papaya, peeled and diced
1/3 cup fresh pineapple, diced
1/4 cup red bell peppers, diced
1/3 cup tomatoes, seeded and diced
1/4 cup water chestnuts, diced
3 green onions, chopped
1/4 cup cilantro, chopped
1 teaspoon Hawaiian rock salt
Juice of 2 limes
1 Hawaiian chili pepper, seeded and chopped

Dice all the fruit about the same size and mix with bell pepper, tomato, water chestnuts, green onions, cilantro, salt, and lime juice. Add Hawaiian chili pepper to taste, and mix well. Pour into jar; cover and refrigerate. Will keep for about a week in the refrigerator.

—*Originally appeared in* Homemade Gifts of Sweets & Treats

Papaya Salsa

Makes about 1-1/2 cups

1 large, firm-ripe papaya, peeled, seeded, and cubed
1 large red bell pepper, grilled and diced
2 teaspoons fresh mint leaves, chopped
1 tablespoon fresh cilantro, chopped
2 tablespoons fresh lime juice

Combine all ingredients; gently toss together until mixed well. Serve with broiled, baked, or fried fish.

—Originally appeared in Homemade Gifts of Sweets & Treats

SAUCES
&
MARINADES

Sushi Rice Vinegar Sauce

Makes 1 cup

3-1/4 cups Japanese rice vinegar
4-1/2 cups sugar (decrease, if desired)
1/4 cup salt

Combine ingredients and heat in saucepan over low heat until sugar and salt dissolve. Cool. Store in covered bottle in a cool place. Use over hot cooked rice for sushi.

For Sushi Rice: Use 1 cup sushi rice vinegar to 5 cups hot cooked rice. Cook only as much rice as you will need each time. Pour over hot rice; toss gently to mix. Do not mix with circular motions. Cool.

—*Originally appeared in* Homemade Gifts of Sweets & Treats

Stir-Fry Sauces
Makes about 1/3 cup sauce

Stir-frying is a great way to serve nutritional dishes relatively inexpensively as the expensive meats are extended with various vegetables. This is also a fast way to get dinner on the table.

Sesame Soy Sauce
1-1/2 teaspoons cornstarch
2 teaspoons rice vinegar
1/3 cup chicken broth
2 tablespoons soy sauce
1 tablespoon sugar
1 tablespoon minced green onion
2 tablespoons toasted sesame seeds
2 teaspoons sesame oil
1/2 teaspoon minced garlic

Chinese Black Bean Sauce
1-1/2 teaspoons cornstarch
1-1/2 teaspoons sherry
1/2 cup chicken broth
1-1/2 tablespoons Chinese black bean/garlic sauce
1 tablespoon sugar
1 teaspoon Asian chili paste
1/2 teaspoon minced fresh ginger root

Cantonese Orange or Lemon Sauce

1-1/2 teaspoons cornstarch
2 teaspoons soy sauce
1/3 cup chicken broth
2 tablespoons orange or lemonade concentrate
2 tablespoons sherry
1-1/2 teaspoons oyster sauce
1 teaspoon sugar
1/2 teaspoon minced fresh ginger

Whisk together cornstarch with the second ingredient until well-blended then whisk in the remaining ingredients; pour into the stir-fry mixture, stirring well to coat evenly and cook until gravy thickens, about 15 seconds. Transfer the stir-fry dish to a bowl and serve immediately.

Suggested Stir-Fry Mixtures:

- Chicken with shiitake mushrooms, broccoli, carrots and sugar snap peas with sesame soy sauce
- Pork with shiitake mushrooms, asparagus, red onions, carrots and bok choy with Chinese black bean sauce
- Shrimp with onion, bell pepper wedges, pineapple chunks and shiitake mushrooms with Cantonese orange or lemon sauce

—*Originally appeared in*
Hawai'i Cooks & Saves

Korean Barbecue Sauce

Makes about 1 quart

A "standard" sauce for Korean barbecued dishes such as Kalbi and Kun Koki. It may also be used as a marinade for chicken or pork.

2 cups soy sauce
1-1/2 cups sugar
1/2 cup toasted sesame seeds
1/2 cup canola oil
3/4 cup minced onion
1/2 cup minced green onion
2 cloves garlic, crushed
1 piece (1/2 inch) ginger, crushed
1 teaspoon fresh ground pepper
1 teaspoon sesame oil

Combine all ingredients in jar; cover and refrigerate. Shake well before using as marinade for meats and poultry.

—Originally appeared in Hawai'i Cooks & Saves

Maple Barbecue Sauce

Makes about 3 cups

Everyone enjoys a good barbecue in which the "secret ingredient" is the sauce. Here's one that "you'll enjoy once your try it"—it is one of my favorites as I enjoy the subtle flavor of maple and it has a little "kick" to it.

1-1/3 cup ketchup
2/3 cup cider vinegar
1/2 cup maple syrup
1/2 cup canola or olive oil
1 tablespoon Dijon mustard
1/2 teaspoon garlic salt
1 teaspoon Worcestershire sauce
1/2 teaspoon chili powder
1/2 teaspoon cayenne*
Dash hot pepper sauce*

Combine all ingredients in a quart jar; stir to combine or cover and shake vigorously until well combined. Use as marinade or glaze for meats and poultry.

*Decrease or delete if you don't like a spicy sauce.

—*Originally appeared in* Hawai'i Cooks & Saves

Hawaiian Barbecue Sauce

Makes 6 cups

2 cups olive oil
1 cup ketchup
1 cup soy sauce
1/2 cup brown sugar, packed
2 tablespoons salt
1 cup chopped onions
3 cloves garlic, crushed
1 teaspoon fresh ginger, minced
1 tablespoon chili sauce

Mix all ingredients in a saucepan. Bring to a boil, stirring occasionally. Reduce heat and simmer about 30 to 45 minutes.

—Originally appeared in Homemade Gifts of Sweets & Treats

Teriyaki Sauce Marinade

Makes 2 cups

1 cup soy sauce
1/2 cup water
1/4 cup mirin
1/2 cup brown sugar, packed
1/2 cup sugar
1 tablespoon garlic, minced
1 tablespoon fresh ginger, minced

Combine ingredients in a saucepan and heat until the sugars dissolve. Cool marinade before using. This recipe makes enough to marinate 3 to 4 pounds of meat.

—Originally appeared in Hawai'i Cooks & Saves

Tartar Sauce

Makes about 1 cup

Tartar Sauce is a must for Hawai'i's fried fish and seafood dishes...and easy to make.

1 cup mayonnaise
1 tablespoon minced onion
1 tablespoon minced sweet pickle
1 teaspoon minced green olives, optional

Combine all ingredients; mix thoroughly. Serve with seafood.

—Originally appeared in Hawai'i Cooks & Saves

Brown Mushroom Sauce

Makes about 14 cups

Hawai'i loves brown gravy poured over almost everything and this sauce can also be served as gravy over your favorite meat dishes and roasts.

3 tablespoons butter or margarine
1 can (2 oz.) mushroom stems and pieces, drained
3 tablespoons flour
1/4 teaspoon salt
Dash of ground pepper
Few drops Worcestershire sauce
1/2 cup consommé or beef or chicken broth
1/2 cup water

Melt butter in saucepan over low heat; add mushrooms, flour and seasonings and brown; add consommé and water gradually while stirring constantly. Cook until thickened. Sauce may be thickened with more flour and additional seasonings may also be added as desired (i.e., garlic salt, marjoram powders and bay leaf).

—*Originally appeared in* Hawai'i Cooks & Saves

CONDIMENTS

Green Chili Relish

Makes 2 quarts

3 (7 oz.) cans diced green chilies, drained
3 (4-1/2 oz.) cans chopped black olives
1 bunch green onions, chopped
3 medium tomatoes, peeled and chopped
1/2 cup olive oil
1/2 cup white wine vinegar
1/2 teaspoon garlic salt

Combine green chilies and black olives; mix until well blended. Add green onions and tomatoes. Mix olive oil, vinegar, and garlic salt. Pour over first 4 ingredients; mix well. Store in covered jars in refrigerator. Stir or shake occasionally. Serve with chips or crackers.

—*Originally appeared in* Homemade Gifts of Sweets & Treats

Household Mustard

Makes 1/2 pint

1-1/4 cups water
2 teaspoons sea salt
3 tablespoons white mustard seeds
1/2 cup white wine vinegar
Salt and pepper to taste

Boil water and sea salt in small saucepan; remove from heat and let stand until lukewarm. In a medium bowl, pour warm salt water over mustard seeds; let stand 12 hours; drain. Crush seeds until soft and creamy with a wooden spoon. Bring vinegar to boil in small saucepan; gradually add to mustard. Add salt and pepper to taste. Spoon into washed and sterilized 1/2-pint jar. Seal tightly. Let mature several days before using. Will keep up to 1 month.

—*Originally appeared in* Homemade Gifts of Sweets & Treats

Tarragon Mustard

Makes 2-1/2 cups

4 ounces dry mustard
5/8 cup white vinegar
5/8 cup tarragon vinegar
3 eggs
1-1/2 cups granulated or brown sugar
2 teaspoons salt
1 tablespoon dried tarragon

Combine dry mustard and vinegars in a blender. Beat eggs
with sugar, salt, and tarragon. Whisk vinegar-mustard
mixture into egg mixture and cook over low heat until thickened. Cool. Pour into sterilized jars.

—*Originally appeared in* Homemade Gifts of Sweets & Treats

Fresh Herb-Flavored Olive Oil

Makes 2 cups

1 cup fresh herb leaves and stems (basil, parsley, mint, tarragon, rosemary, or thyme)
2 cups olive oil

Wash and dry herb leaves and stems well. Place herbs in wide-necked jar with tight fitting lid; fill with olive oil of your choice. Close tightly. Store 2 to 3 weeks in cool, dark place. Strain oil into another jar or bottle. Add sprigs of herbs to the oil before sealing. Store in refrigerator.

—*Originally appeared in* Homemade Gifts of Sweets & Treats

Cilantro Pesto

Makes about 1-1/2 cups

1 ounce macadamia nuts, chopped
1 tablespoon lime juice
2 cups fresh cilantro, chopped
1/2 cup virgin olive oil
1 teaspoon chopped garlic
1 teaspoon chopped ginger
Salt and white pepper to taste

In a food processor or blender, blend all ingredients together at high speed until smooth. Serve with seafood.

—Originally appeared in Homemade Gifts of Sweets & Treats

RUBS, SALTS & MIXES

Creole Seasoning

Makes 1/2 cup

2 tablespoons freshly grated black pepper
2 tablespoons ground white pepper
2 tablespoons paprika
1 tablespoon confectioners' sugar
1 tablespoon salt
1 tablespoon garlic powder
2 teaspoons dried oregano
1 teaspoon ground thyme
1 teaspoon cayenne pepper
1/2 teaspoon ground celery seeds

Combine ingredients in a mixing bowl; stir well. Store in air-tight container.

—*Originally appeared in* Homemade Gifts of Sweets & Treats

Char Siu Dry Rub

Makes 6 cups

6 cups sugar
1/2 cup hoisin sauce
1/3 cup red bean curd (nam yui)
1 teaspoon red food coloring (Chinese paste-type found in
   Chinatown)

Combine all ingredients; mix well. Store in covered jar in a
cool place.

When ready to use, place meat or poultry in large plastic bag
and sprinkle with dry rub; seal well; let stand 15 minutes. The
juices from the meat will create a sauce. Using
disposable gloves, rub entire surface
of meat thoroughly with sauce
and marinate meat in sealed
bag overnight or up to 2 to 3
days in refrigerator.

Suggested Meats:
Spareribs, pork loin,
pork butt, chicken,
duck, turkey

—Originally appeared in Homemade Gifts of Sweets & Treats

Curry and Green Chili Mix

Makes about 1/2 cup

1 teaspoon whole cloves
2 tablespoons cumin seed
1/4 cup curry powder
1 to 2 jalapeños, seeded and minced
2 tablespoons Hawaiian rock salt

Toast cloves and cumin in skillet over medium heat until cumin browns slightly; grind coarsely in grinder or mortar and pestle. Combine all ingredients in a bowl; toss well and store, covered, in a glass jar. Rub this on pork, duck, or chicken before roasting or sprinkle on grilled vegetables.

—*Originally appeared in* Homemade Gifts of Sweets & Treats

Spicy Seasoned Salt

Makes about 8 cups

5 pounds Hawaiian rock salt
1/3 cup coarse black pepper
1/3 cup chopped garlic
1/3 cup grated fresh ginger
Crushed chili pepper to taste

Combine salt and pepper in large roasting pan; mix well. Add garlic and ginger using back of large wooden spoon to mix well and smash pieces. Bake at 350°F for 20 to 30 minutes, stirring every 2 to 3 minutes, or until slightly brown and dry. Cool thoroughly and store in covered jar in a cool place. Great on broiled or baked meats, fish, seafood, and poultry. May also be used to flavor soups and stews.

—Originally appeared in Homemade Gifts of Sweets & Treats

Sweet 'n Salty Seasoning Salt

Makes about 3-1/2 cups

2 cups Hawaiian rock salt
1-1/2 cups brown sugar, packed
1-1/2 tablespoons peppercorns, coarsely ground
1-1/4 teaspoons garlic powder

Combine all ingredients. Store in covered jar in a cool place. Use to season meats, poultry, fish, seafood, etc., when baking or broiling only, not frying.

—Originally appeared in
Homemade Gifts of Sweets & Treats

Herb Blend

Makes about 3/4 cup

3 tablespoons dried whole basil
3 tablespoons dried whole marjoram
3 tablespoons dried whole thyme
3 tablespoons dried whole tarragon
1 tablespoon dried lemon peel
2 tablespoons dried whole oregano

Place all ingredients in a small jar; cover and shake until mixture is completely blended.

—*Originally appeared in* Homemade Gifts of Sweets & Treats

Rosemary Salt Mix

Makes about 12 ounces

1/2 pound sea salt
2 ounces fresh rosemary, finely ground
2 ounces black pepper, finely ground

Combine all ingredients and mix until well blended. Store in airtight jar in cool place. Use to season meats and poultry.

—*Originally appeared in* Homemade Gifts of Sweets & Treats

Glossary

'ahi—Hawaiian name for yellowfin or bigeye tuna

guava—yellow thin-skinned fruit with a slightly acetic pulp

Hawaiian rock salt—coarse sea salt

hoisin sauce—Chinese soybean sauce used as condiment or for flavoring

Kahlua—coffee flavored liqueur

kumquat—strong flavored citrus fruit

lychee—juicy, white, round, sweet fruit covered with rough, red skin

mango—sweet, aromatic fruit, tastes like a slightly resinous peach.

miso—Japanese fermented soybean paste

nam yui—Chinese fermented red bean curd

papaya—sweet, yellow/green pear-shaped tropical fruit

passion fruit—aka liliko'i—tough-skin, egg-shaped fruit with seedy pulp

shichimi togarashi—Japanese term for mixed chili pepper

wasabi powder—Japanese name for powdered horseradish